SNAKES WITH VENOM

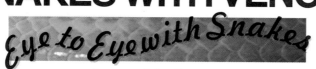

Eye to Eye with Snakes

Lynn M. Stone

The Rourke Book Company, Inc.
Vero Beach, Florida 32964

PHOTO CREDITS
© Joe McDonald: p.6, 17; © J.H. Pete Carmichael:
p.16, 19; © Lynn M. Stone: cover, title page, p.4, 9,
10, 13, 14, 20

EDITORIAL SERVICES
Penworthy Learning Systems

Library of Congress Cataloging-in-Publication Data

Stone, Lynn M.
    Snakes with venom / Lynn M. Stone.
        p. cm. — (Eye to eye with snakes)
    Summary: Describes venomous snakes of the world, including
cobras, rattlesnakes, coral snakes, and pit vipers.
        ISBN 1-55916-259-7
            1. Elapidae—Juvenile literature. [1. Poisonous snakes. 2.snakes]
I. Title.

QL666.064 S76 2000
597.96'4—dc21   00-025035

1-55916-259-7

Printed in the USA

CONTENTS

VENOMOUS SNAKES

Venomous snakes make a powerful poison called **venom**. **Venomous** snakes use this poison to kill the animals they eat. Venomous snakes also use venom to defend themselves.

The bite of a venomous snake is painful and dangerous to humans. The bite of many venomous snakes can be deadly. Snake bites cause hundreds of human deaths every year throughout the world. North America's venomous snakes, however, rarely kill humans.

The timber rattlesnake appeared on early American flags with the slogan, "Don't Tread on Me." That's still good advice.

Different kinds of snakes make different kinds of venom. There are two general types of venom. One type works largely to destroy flesh and healthy blood. The other type works largely to destroy nerves and muscle control.

A snake's venom is usually more deadly to certain animals than others. The eastern diamond-back rattlesnake, for example, produces venom that is more deadly to rabbits than rats.

A snake makes venom in special glands in its jaws. The snake's venom is carried to its victims through its bite.

A western diamondback rattlesnake, jaws wide open, strikes out. The snake's striking reach is about half its body length.

Venomous snakes of one kind or another are found on every continent except Antarctica. Only in Australia, however, are there more **species**, or kinds, of venomous snakes than **nonvenomous** ones.

The Australian death adder has the diamond-shaped head typical of vipers. But the highly venomous death adder is an elapid, one of many in Australia.

ELAPIDS

You know them as cobras, mambas, kraits, and coral snakes. **Herpetologists**, the snake scientists, know them together as **elapids**. Some herpetologists include sea snakes in the elapid family.

The elapids and sea snakes are a group of more than 250 species. Their venom is the type that attacks nerves.

Like another family of venomous snakes, the vipers, elapids have sharp, hollow front teeth. Each front tooth, or fang, has a tiny opening at its tip.

America's only elapids are the coral snake species of the Southeast and Southwest. See a bigger, more deadly elapid, the green mamba, on title page.

The snake's venom travels through the hollow fang into whatever prey the snake bites. The longer an elapid bites, the more venom it can inject into a bite wound.

Coral snakes are the only elapids found in the United States. Elapids are more common in Africa and Asia. In Australia, they are the most common snakes.

Gaboon viper shows the typical diamond-shaped head of true viper. This is the biggest of the true vipers, reaching a length of seven feet (over 2 meters).

COBRAS

The most famous elapids are the cobras of Asia and Africa. Many cobras flatten their head and neck into a "hood." The hood makes a cobra look even more fearsome than it is. Snake charmers keep cobras in baskets.

The king cobra is the largest venomous snake. It can be more than 18 feet (5.5 m) long.

Some cobra species can "spit" their venom at an enemy's eyes. The sprays of venom can cause great eye pain and even blindness. The venom is harmless on unbroken skin.

The king cobra is the largest venomous snake on earth, reaching 18 feet (5.5 meters) in length. Yet the king cobra is no match for the little mongoose.

*An Indian cobra spreads its hood in a threatening pose.
The Indian cobra probably kills more people in India than
any other venomous snake.*

This black and white cobra of South Africa is one of several cobra species that can "spit" venom through the open tips of their fangs.

VIPERS

Vipers have a somewhat different way of delivering their venom. A viper's hollow fangs inject venom quickly in a deep, stabbing bite. The venom of vipers attacks blood and flesh more than nerves.

For its size, a viper has longer, more curved fangs than an elapid. When it bites, a viper opens its mouth wide and raises its fangs from the roof of its mouth. After biting, a viper folds its fangs back into its mouth.

A viper couldn't close its mouth if its long fangs were fixed in place like an elapid's fangs.

The vipers of North and South America are **pit vipers**.

Rattlesnake skull shows the remarkably long, hollow fangs typical of vipers.

They have an organ in their heads that senses the body heat of their prey. That organ lies in an opening, or pit, between the snake's nostrils and eyes. North American pit vipers are the copperheads, cottonmouths, and rattlesnakes.

RATTLESNAKES

Rattlesnakes are pit vipers found only in the Americas. They are the only snakes with the feature called a rattle.

A rattlesnake's rattle looks much like a row of fat, horn-colored buttons. It's found at the end of the snake's tail.

By rapidly moving the rattle, a rattlesnake makes a loud buzzing noise. That sound can warn larger animals not to step on the snake. But beware! A rattlesnake does not always rattle.

Hard scales make "horns" over the eyes of the desert sand viper. The "horns" help keep eye coverings sand free in the North African deserts.

GLOSSARY

elapids (EL uh pudz) – Snakes that belong to this family of venomous snakes: cobras, kraits, mambas, coral snakes and their kin

herpetologists (her puh TAHL uh jistz) – people who study reptiles and/or amphibians

non-venomous (nahn VEN uh mus) – refers to a snake that does not produce venom, a poison

pit viper (PIT VI per) – any one of several kinds of venomous snakes that have a heat-sensing organ in an opening (pit) in their head

species (SPEE sheez) – within a group of closely related animals, such as rattlesnakes, one certain type (*tiger* rattlesnake)

venom (VEN um) – the poison produced by certain animals, especially certain snakes

venomous (VEN uh mus) – refers to a snake that produces venom, a poison

FURTHER READING

Find out more about snakes with these helpful books:

Greer, Dr. Allen. **Reptiles**, Time Life, 1996

McCarthy, Colin. **Reptile**. Alfred Knopf, 1991

Schnieper, Claudia. **Snakes, Silent Hunters**. Carolrhoda, 1995

Simon, Seymor. **Snakes**. Harper Collins, 1994

INDEX